TOWAR   Г

Prayers thro

Denis Duncan

SPCK

First published in Great Britain in 2009

Society for Promoting Christian Knowledge
36 Causton Street
London SW1P 4ST

British Library Cataloguing-in-Publication Data
A catalogue record for this book is available from the British Library

ISBN 978–0–281–06141–9

1 3 5 7 9 10 8 6 4 2

Typeset by Graphicraft Limited, Hong Kong
Printed in Great Britain by CPI Bookmarque Ltd, Croydon, Surrey

Produced on paper from sustainable forests

Contents

Preface   v

Acknowledgements   vii

Days 1–10: Towards the darkness   1

Days 11–16: The crisis   23

Days 17–40: Towards the light   37

Afterword   86

Notes   87

iii

Preface

Early in 2007 I suffered three crises, each of which was serious enough to threaten my future. The first was a financial one – an extremely major fraud perpetrated by someone whom I trusted and to whom I had given substantial help. The second was a property disaster, a water leak that various experts could not trace and the implications of which were, from both a financial and a property point of view, simply horrendous. The third crisis was of a personal nature. It also had serious implications for my future.

In a long life and ministry, I had faced many challenging situations, knowingly accepted back-to-the-wall undertakings, and even rather prided myself on coping with whatever life threw at me. The coincidence of these three crises, at my stage in life – I was in my mid-eighties – was just too much, and I suffered a major health breakdown (for the first time in my life).

At crisis point, I voluntarily entered the mental health unit of a London hospital, where depression was diagnosed. As the episode was regarded as 'very severe', I was in hospital for three and a half months. I was discharged, having made 'a very good recovery'.

I have now resumed my ministry, or at least that aspect of it which, at 89, I can realistically undertake, my writing ministry.

Seeing this whole experience as, in spiritual terms, a 'dark night of the soul', I have written these prayers to help, and especially encourage, others who are going through similar darkness and to emphasize the possibility of a return to the light. I have therefore contracted what took some six months to go through into the scriptural concept of '40 days and 40 nights', dividing that time into three clear phases: first the downhill phase 'towards the darkness', second the crisis, and then the third phase 'towards the light'. The third part is the important part, as it is this section which makes the book what it is intended to be, very positive indeed. Depression can be overcome.

The rediscovery of my ability to write, and its expression in concrete work, and in particular this book, was and is of fundamental importance to my recovery. I have therefore made that central to the final positive sequence. I realize that what has been so vital in my case will not connect with some readers. What is important is that whoever reads these prayers will seek to recognize whatever is the central focus in their own lives, a focus which depression has destroyed, and which, if rediscovered, will be a testimony to the healing process at work in them. My experience with my particular talent will, I hope, be your experience with yours.

It is the purpose of this book to tell you that you *can* pass through the dark night and reach the light.

Acknowledgements

I want to record my great debt to my daughter, Carol Pyle, who carried the very heavy burden of dealing with all my business affairs, including the property problem, when I was totally unable as well as unwilling to do so; to my son, Raymond, who also helped with the property situation; and to 'my closest friend', Jillian Tallon, who was 'always there', in the darkness, through the crisis and on the journey towards the light. To which I add, *Deo gratias*.

Days 1–10
Towards the darkness

Day 1

Morning

For the gift of a new day, I thank you, O God. It comes with mixed feelings, hope, expectation and anticipation. But apprehension, too, Lord. For that, forgive me.

I have always believed in your providential care; that, loving you and you loving me, 'all things will work together for good'; that you are truly 'God with us', God with *me*. Why should I be afraid? But I am, Lord, I don't know why.

Your Word is crystal clear. 'Let not your heart be troubled.' This was said to your disciples and so to all of us; 'neither let it be afraid'. Why? Because you promise us the gift of peace, your peace that 'the world can neither give nor take away'. I have known that peace and, because of it, have always tried to dismiss troubles and fear. I try to do that now, for your Word must be obeyed.

Grant me the grace to succeed, Lord.

Evening

For peaceful sleep and untroubled dreams, I pray to you, O God. But ere I sleep I want to reflect on the great truths of my faith . . . the unfailing providence I know so well, the glory of the Incarnation, that is 'the Word made flesh', the wonder of the Resurrection, the coming of the Holy Spirit. I give you thanks for (as your servant Paul called them) the 'deep roots and firm foundations'[1] on which I stand. How greatly these convictions have sustained me over so many years. Let them sustain me now, I pray.

So, knowing that yours is a love that just will not let us go, in quietness and confidence, I lie down to sleep.

Day 2

Morning

A new day, and so a new beginning. I give you thanks, Lord, that whatever has happened in the past, however awful have been my failures, you always offer me that new beginning. How glorious is that tenet of our faith: 'I believe in the forgiveness of sins.' The 'how' and 'why' of all that makes possible the gift of your forgiveness lies beyond my understanding. All I know is that, in some mysterious way, it was for us, for me, Jesus 'hung and suffered there'.

I value beyond words this glorious truth. It means that I can begin again, clean sheet, clean slate. My 'scarlet sins' (as your prophet Isaiah called them) are made 'white as snow'.[2] Redeemed, I can go forward, my hope renewed. And so I do, Lord.

Evening

The tensions of the day have come and gone, Lord, but problems making their subtle presence felt have disturbed me. I feel that unconscious anxiety is breaking through into my conscious mind, and it worries me. There are things that are going to have to be faced. It is with these things on my mind, I prepare for rest. As the old hymn says: 'I need thee, oh, I need thee.'

I turn to the psalmist again, O God, and am reassured. He sings of your presence around us wherever we are. I hear his words: 'You hem me in – behind and before: you have laid your hand upon me', he says.[3] So I can say, hearing this: 'I know whom I have believed and am persuaded that you are able to do whatever I have committed to you'.[4]

As you told the Israelites to 'go forward', I go forward with hope. There is so much that needs to be changed in the world. Help me to try to do it. There is so much to read that is enhancing. Help me to find it. There is so much to learn. Help me to seek it.

So may I end this day with my mind stretched, my heart uplifted, my soul restored.

And enjoy peaceful sleep.

Day 3

Morning

I awake to greet another day with hope in my heart, Lord. But there is so much to face in our world today – the impartiality of misfortune, the risk of accident, natural disasters, the wickedness of so-called 'human' beings. How evil men – and women – can be! Murder, rape, violence, abuse; the daily news is of wars and rumours of war, widespread starvation for many, spreading disease. And so much more, Lord.

The world is (as John Baillie put it) 'a good thing spoiled'.[5] You created the world and it was good, but the primal sin of pride corrupted it and has polluted it. I find it hard to face this world today, Lord.

But this is where I have to be, so I pray for courage, strength and grace to help me bring some good back into the world which you created in love, the world in which Jesus lived and taught and healed, the world for which he died and is risen.

So strengthened, I face life in this world, believing that you – being, as I recall again, 'God with us' – will make all things well.

Evening

Constant, O God, is the tension between the burden of the world's evil ways and my conviction that 'you hold the whole world in your hands'. I take my rest assured of your providential care. Yet I am ill at ease within.

Why is it, Lord, I feel that there are wounds unhealed? Why are secret fears beginning to surface within me? Are there people in whom I am losing faith? I am committed to trust you, Lord, but I sense doubts are stirring within me.

Tell me again that you are indeed 'Immanuel, God with us', that I am not alone, that wherever I go, you will be there. 'If I go up to the heavens, you are there,' the psalmist tells me.

> If I make my bed in the depths, you are there.
> If I rise on the wings of the dawn,
> if I settle on the far side of the sea,
> even there your hand will guide me . . .
> If I say, 'Surely, the darkness will hide me . . .'
> the night will shine like the day,
> for darkness is as light to you.[6]

How wonderfully the psalmist speaks.
Reassured, I lie down to sleep, Lord.

Day 4

Morning

Thank you, O God, for those comforting words before I fell asleep last night. I wake up encouraged, strengthened, renewed, ready for whatever today may bring. The problems that lurk around me are still there. Worries wait in the wings. But the knowledge that I am not alone as I face them will help me tackle them positively and creatively. It is so often in the darkness that blessings come. For what you gave me yesterday, Lord, I give you thanks today.

'I press toward the mark for the prize of the high calling of God in Christ Jesus.' Those words of your servant Paul[7] have sustained me through the years and I want to live them now. To fulfil my vocation is my dearest wish, to serve you as you deserve my utmost desire. Whatever the lurking pain, I will go forward this day fighting but not heeding the wounds, toiling but not seeking for rest, labouring and asking for no reward except that I do your will.

Evening

As night draws near, Lord, my sense of apprehension grows. Let 'no ill dreams disturb my rest'. I do not want to lie awake for hours, pondering the anxiety I feel. How I need to remember those words I came to know so long ago:

> Let me no more my comfort draw
> From my frail hold of thee.
> In this alone rejoice with awe –
> Thy mighty grasp of me.

To know that helps me, Lord.

O God, I ask you to bless the work I try to do for you. For so many years it has been my calling to minister to people in your name. Thank

8

you for sustaining me through the years, often bringing good results from unpromising situations and for helping me when I became discouraged, reminding me to 'keep looking unto Jesus', the author of our faith. How often the familiar words of a seaside mission chorus go through my mind:

Turn your eyes upon Jesus
Look full on his wonderful face,
And the cares of earth will grow strangely dim
In the light of his glory and grace.

Thank you for today, Lord. You have helped me so much that I can now 'lay me down in peace'.

Day 5

Morning

I begin the day, Lord, where I always do and that is 'at the throne of grace'. I make known to you my earnest prayers . . . for people in need, for peace in the world, for the easing of suffering, for the upholding of the name of Jesus. I do this out of obedience. That we should 'pray without ceasing' is your will. But I also pray out of need, for without your sustaining grace I can do nothing. I pray in the belief that you are the God who hears our prayers. And by that faith I live.

But doubt constantly invades my mind, Lord. The sick I prayed for are not healed. I laid before you my problems, but solutions have not come. I prayed for the growth of your Church, but it declines. I asked for conflicts to cease, but they multiply. Don't you hear my prayers, Lord? Why do the answers I seek not come? Are you there, Lord?

So many questions flood my mind, Lord. Am I praying in a wrong and unacceptable way? Am I concerned only with *my* needs and desires? Should I be asking for bigger, less trivial things – remembering that there's 'a wideness in your mercy like the wideness of the sea'? Am I, as you made known through your Word, praying, believing I shall receive? For your promise is that, so asking, I shall receive. Did I not ask in Jesus' name . . . yet I know that that is essential in my prayers? These questions will be with me through this day, Lord.

Grant me illumination, Lord.

Evening

It is evening time, but can I pray? The questions haunting me all day are with me still. Why are my prayers not answered, Lord?

I seek for understanding. It is not many words but sincerity which you require. You want a 'humble and contrite heart', but this I have.

Have I faith 'like a grain of mustard seed', a faith that can 'move mountains'? I have such faith. And I do ask everything 'in Jesus' name', believing I shall receive.

I must take Jesus at his word: 'Whatever you ask for in my name, I will do it,' he said.[8]

Let me then try to pray, Lord:

I pray for the coming of your kingdom, as first I should.

I pray for your Church that it may proclaim your Word 'with boldness'.

I pray for family and friends, for all who are ill, all who are dispirited and depressed; for all who are in hospital, hospices and places of care, and for those who look after them.

I pray for myself, my needs, my honest desires.

I place my worries, problems and fears within your care.

'Hear my prayer, O Lord, and let my cry come unto thee'.[9]

And with that prayer, I look for peaceful sleep.

Day 6

Morning

'Be still and know that I am God.' God, I believe the truth of these words from Psalm 46 and, with them, I go forward into this day.

But I feel a tension within me, Lord. I cling to faith and hope, but I have increasing doubts. Why is my faith failing me? And failing you? Or am I just doing what I should not do, being 'troubled and afraid'?

But there is reality in my apprehension, Lord. Situations are developing that are too big for me to handle. There are people who seek to cause me pain and do me down. I face a future that is ominous and threatening.

'All will be truly well,' said Julian of Norwich. But it isn't, Lord.

Where can I find encouragement? Let me meditate on your servant Nehemiah, whom you commanded to rebuild the broken-down walls of Jerusalem, the 'holy city'. Faced by chaos so great that there was no path along which his ass could go, Nehemiah made a decision. It was to face the reality of the situation and start from there. Help me, Lord, to do just that. My life is not easy or trouble-free: the problems are real. There are worrying issues before me. There are troublesome people too. There are decisions that need to be made now. Grant me the strength to face all these things today.

I am where I am, O God. I start from here.

Evening

I try to deal effectively with the difficulties that face me. I have sought to follow Nehemiah's example and face the realities that are in front of me, Lord. I have also tried to cope with unwelcome murmurings of apprehension within my heart by saying the words given to us by your servant Paul about 'the peace that passes

12

understanding', the peace that comes when 'hearts and minds' are filled with love (heart) and knowledge (mind) 'through Christ Jesus'.[10] How true these words are. Our wholeness involves our whole being, mind *and* heart, the intellectual *and* the emotional, our thoughts *and* our feelings.

I seek to hold strongly to that peace, Lord, for I sense conflict within me is developing into something worse, a battle for my soul.

O God, it is imperative that I hold on to the things 'most surely believed'. My ability to believe is on trial. My faith is being severely tested. Surround me with your embracing grace as I echo the words of your servant Peter, sinking into the Sea of Galilee: 'Save me, Lord, or I perish.'

Day 7

Morning

I prayed last night, 'O God, save me or I perish', your servant Peter's anguished cry as he tried to walk on the water. It was a cry from the heart. Did you hear me, Lord?

I am trying to understand what is happening to me, Lord. I ask again: are you putting me to the test? You taught us to say: 'Let us not go into temptation.' That means, I am sure, a time of testing. You surely do not 'lead us into temptation' but it may be your will that, for a season, we go through a time of testing. Is this such a time, Lord? Are you questioning the quality of my faith, wondering if it will stand up to such examination? Is this a time of catharsis, of cleansing, of stripping? It seems to me that it is.

I feel the strain, Lord. I do not know if I can cope with such a time, for my sense of your presence seems to diminish daily. Have you forsaken me, O God? Is the covenant of grace (on your part) and faith (on my part) breaking down? Irretrievably?

It is enough. I must take hold of myself, Lord, recall what I believe and be strong.

Therefore, through this day, support me in my fight for faith, I pray. Tell me that you 'will not leave me nor forsake me' but that you will be 'God with me'. My need is great: your grace is greater.

For that I thank you, O God.

Evening

The day is far spent and evening comes, a day of struggle behind me. Trying to deal with worldly things has made me anxious about spiritual matters. I look at all that constitutes my present life . . . problem situations, people in whom I am losing faith, tension within; and I fear lest this is a time of testing or of punishment for, as the psalmist says, 'My sin is ever before me.'[11]

14

It is not easy, Lord, to look inwards and acknowledge the dismal failures of the past. They are many; they are great. I confess the things that I have done and should not have done. I ponder the things not done that I should have done. I shudder that even my best intentions can be corrupted by the sheer power of 'original sin'.

I turn to the psalmist again, Lord, and cry out: 'Create within me a clean heart, O God; and renew a right spirit within me. Cast me not away from thy presence; and take not thy holy spirit from me!'[12] If there has been that 'wrong spirit' within me, if I have misused your gifts and lost your trust in me, forgive me, Lord.

I ask again for peaceful sleep and for freedom from unhappy dreams. And so, I wait on you this night, my soul does wait, and in your Word do I hope.

Day 8

Morning

How hard that night was to cope with, Lord! Sleep would not come. I lay awake and worried greatly over the problems all around me. But I feel a sense of guilt that I am 'troubled and afraid'. For those who have faith in you should not feel fear. How can I resolve this conflict within me, Lord?

Help me, O God, as this day begins, to take firm hold again of the faith that I have known through many years. 'In the world ye shall have tribulation,' Jesus said, 'but be of good cheer; I have overcome the world.'[13] Yours is the victory. Can it be mine, Lord?

I put my trust in those words today. It is of the essence of my faith to believe that you have overcome sin and death and evil and your victory, by grace, we share.

Encouraged, Lord, I set aside worry, anxiety and 'the sin that does so easily beset us', and embrace your power to get me up and to go on. My only hope is your strength. The only peace I have is the peace that you so graciously give.

Thus blessed, I go on my way.

Evening

O God, as this day ends, I confess that I grow weary of life. Battered by circumstances, bewildered by people and the things they do to hurt, bruised by guilt within, I cannot feel hope for the future. If the days are all anxiety, and there is no rest at night, how can I live and work and minister? All I can do is exist.

But you say, again through your servant Paul, that 'our light affliction is but for a moment'. It does not feel like that, Lord. The night is long and very dark.

But I ask you, Lord, to dismiss such thinking from my mind. There is so much that is good and lovely and 'of good report' in the world. There are so many good people. Nor is there any place in the Christian life for such negative and wayward thoughts. Are you there, Lord? I need your help.

For the words of your servant Paul, I give you thanks. He says: 'We are hard pressed on every side, but not crushed; perplexed, but not in despair; persecuted, but not abandoned; struck down, but not destroyed'.[14] Make these words real for me, Lord, so that I have hope.

I give thanks for the sense of victory, despite my darkness, within these words. And so, to my surprise, I go to rest in peace, Lord.

Day 9

Morning

I pray that you will (as your prophet, Hosea, said) draw me to you, this day 'with the cords of love'.[15] I teeter on the brink of doubt and of despair. Renew in me the faith I have known but struggle to retain. I think of your servant Thomas, Lord, 'doubting Thomas'. With the proof of the nail marks on your hands, you convinced him, Lord, but then you said: 'Blessed are those who have not seen and yet have believed'.[16]

So often I seek for proof of your presence, of your capacity to heal, of your wonders and miracles. How great a help it would be to faith to have sight, visible proof of your powers. But this, Lord, is something we must not seek. This is putting you to the test and is forbidden in your Word. So I must cling to faith, blessed in my believing without seeing.

Grant me, Lord, the will to struggle on, to fight fear, to battle against doubt. It is a difficult journey that you ask me to take. But take it I must, so support me, Lord, this day. Where I go, go with me; whatever I try to do, grant me enabling power. I strive for faith and peace. Be with me, Lord.

Evening

'Come unto me, all ye that labour and are heavy laden, and I will give you rest' is your word to us, Lord.[17] How welcome is that invitation as this day ends. I seize and hold on to your promise that we shall find rest for our souls. But rest and peace are hard to come by, Lord. My body is tired, my mind is weary. My soul is heavy.

How can I say 'peace, peace, when there is no peace'? Too many nights of restless endeavour have sapped my strength; heaving and tossing, as anxious thoughts disturb my rest, I have used up my mental strength. Developing doubts over your presence, your failure to answer my prayers, have drained my spiritual strength away. But I must not fail, Lord. I must not give up. I must, by an effort of will, sustain my faith. I must believe.

And so, defying my doubt, I say the Apostles' Creed in reaffirmation of my faith. I murmur the Lord's Prayer to declare my faith in prayer. I whisper the words of benediction, pleading for your blessing.

O ever wakeful, watchful God, who 'will neither slumber nor sleep',[18] I commit myself to your care. Watch over me this night, I pray.

Day 10

Morning

A few hours' sleep, long hours awake: how do I face another day, Lord? And I awake to loneliness, nobody here, nobody near. Are *you* there, Lord?

I do not sense your presence as I used to do. The prayers I offer bring no response, no answer that I seek. Why have you forsaken me, O God, why – I ask again – have you forsaken me?

I do not want to rise and face another day. I do not want to hear the phone. I will not welcome any who come to call. This is desolation indeed.

I am deeply 'troubled', Lord, though I know that I should not be. I am even 'afraid'. For so long I have depended on myself, have always been able to cope with dilemmas and difficulties, competent at overcoming misfortunes, even disasters. But my confidence has gone, Lord. The problems I now face are beyond my control. At my wits' end (as the psalmist says) 'I cry unto the LORD'.[19] But are you there, Lord?

So I face the darkness of this day, resources low, with no peace of mind, just desolation.

Evening

'Nothing can separate us from the love of God in Christ Jesus.' So wrote your servant Paul to the Romans. 'Neither height nor depth nor any other creature . . . nothing'.[20] I want to believe that, Lord. But I can't. All is, yes, desolation.

I cannot work properly because of anxiety. I am not eating as I should. I cannot sleep. I do not want to get up. I am cutting myself off from all family and friends, simply withdrawing from life. And I have lost touch with you, O God. I cannot sense you near.

Is this the dark night of the soul, Lord? Is this the spiritual darkness that saints and mystics have known? I have always sought to do your will, but I can no longer find you. This is my crisis, Lord. Depression, severe depression, the doctors will call it. But it is the spiritual darkness that overwhelms me.

I hear Peter's words again, and feel that they are mine: 'Lord, save me. I am sinking. I am perishing.' My world is collapsing around me.

How can I rest tonight, Lord?

Days 11–16
The crisis

Day 11

Morning

What can I say, Lord? The hour of crisis has come.

Out of the depths I cry to you, O God
I acknowledge my sin: grant me absolution
I acknowledge my sickness: grant me recovery
In Jesus' name, Amen.

Evening

My words are few, Lord. There is so little I can say.

In my darkest hours I wait on you, O God. Are you there, Lord?

Day 12

Morning

How derelict I feel, Lord. How bereft I am of interest in life, in work, in people.

How lacking in faith I am, unable to feel your presence.

I cannot pray, Lord, I cannot worship. I cannot respond to anything. The night is truly dark.

Unsure as I am of your presence with me, Lord, I still give you thanks that those nearest to me try hard to support me, despite my darkened mood. For such consistency and love, I feel grateful. If there is a road to recovery of life and faith, it will be long and very hard, for at this moment I feel no hope. Yet, deep down, I am aware that life must go on, that rejecting life is cowardice, that trying to escape life is futile. It solves nothing.

My frail grasp of you has gone, Lord, and yet still alive within me is the belief, though I do not acknowledge it, that I want your mighty grasp of me to hold.

Evening

It is strange, Lord, I have lost the sense of your presence, even of your being, yet I come to you in prayer. What does this mean, Lord?

As I think in your presence, Lord, I recall your servant J. B. Phillips, telling me that, in his dark night, he had no sense of creativity at all. Nothing in his fruitful life had any reality any more . . . music, literature, the arts, even the Bible he had translated for the benefit of millions. His sense of all lovely things had left him, as had all sense of the holy.

The dark night is long, Lord, and it is lonely. I do not want to see people, talk to them, listen to them. I allow only my nearest and dearest to be in touch, for I am grateful to them. How guilty I feel that my response to them is so poor.

Each night, the medication will give me some sleep but, that blessing given, there comes the hardest part of all, facing another day.

How I hate the morning, Lord! I know that physiologically, depression is at its worst in the early morning. But what alternative is there, except self-destruction, to going on? With an effort of will I stumble through each day, eating because I have to, and between meals, there is only the loneliness I have adopted.

Until the physical darkness of the night approaches, I live with the spiritual darkness of the day.

I cannot pray before I sleep. Belief has gone. Can there truly be a love that 'will not let us go', Lord?

Day 13

Morning

A new day dawns but there is no brightness in it. Is life worthwhile? Is there any future ahead of me?

The practical problems that I face and should deal with remain untouched. The work I ought to do remains undone. The birthdays of which I should take notice are ignored. And all the time I remain withdrawn, alone, my mind wrestling with impossibilities. A sense of impending doom dominates my thoughts and I wrestle constantly with profound guilt. How can I find some peace, Lord?

The hours drag slowly by, motivation dead, enthusism for anything a distant memory. I do not want to read, listen to music, draw or paint, I just want to be alone.

How dark and how lonely is the journey through the dark night. Are you there, Lord?

Evening

And so to sleep, perchance to dream. The prescribed pill will bring both, but will they be troubled dreams? Why is everything in this dark night so negative? But that is the essence of the dark night. It brings 'naught for your comfort'.

I want to pray, Lord. But I can't. I feel let down by your absence, Lord. You did not answer my earnest prayers for help, though they came from my heart. And they were offered 'in Jesus' name'. Were they unacceptable prayers? Was I seeking only my selfish desires? Were they not 'according to your will'? I do not think they were self-centred prayers. They came from the depths of my being. Did you not hear them, Lord?

I ponder these things, but no answer comes. Despair begins its descent upon me. Desolation makes its presence felt. How long, Lord, will this dark night be? How long, Lord?

Afraid to stay awake, fearful of going to sleep lest troubled nightmares come, I am in limbo, Lord. Are you there?

Prayerless, I fall asleep.

Day 14

Morning

Short sleep, long hours awake. My personal darkness persists, Lord. I do not want to get up to meet another day, but I dare not linger here. Some residual sense of reality remains – financial pressure compels me to ring the bank's automatic system to check that balances are safe. If it is not done more problems will arise so I will do it . . . later.

Will there be anyone in touch with me today? Perhaps my family or my closest friend will ring. It is only to them I find it possible to speak. They will not let me down.

Weekdays or Sundays, the days are all the same. The Church feels far off and irrelevant. Would it understand my predicament? I doubt it, Lord, and so the slowly passing hours are spent in unhappy reverie, in battling against insoluble problems. It is all so futile, Lord, but what else can I do? I cannot break through the circle of darkness around me. And so the awful process goes on and on . . . the pondering that never results in action, the wrestling with sin and guilt, the longing for an absent God. What sort of life is this, Lord?

I hear the phone, but let it ring. The door bell too . . . but I do not want to answer it. I want no contact with the outside world.

How long will this dark night persist, Lord?

What desolation . . .

Evening

Evening comes to end a dark day. Nothing has been achieved. No positive thought has crossed my mind. Yet I am tired, physically and mentally, and emotionally weary, spiritually exhausted. Even so, I will not sleep.

The time for evening prayer has come and gone, Lord. Because you do not hear my prayers, what point is there in praying? I have implored your help with pressing problems, but no answer comes. Are you not there, Lord?

I feel forsaken, Lord, and I am angry. I do as you ask: I pray in Jesus' name, I ask believing I shall receive, but all to no avail. I take refuge in self-pity. Why should all this happen to me, Lord? I have served you all these years, yet now I find myself alone, abandoned, derelict. It feels unfair, Lord.

If I do not sleep, Lord, how can I live? If I find no rest, Lord, can I even exist?

And beyond whatever hours of sleep may come, I dread the waking up. 'O wretched man that I am', your servant Paul said. 'Who shall deliver me from the body of this death?'[21] He found an answer, but I find none.

You are not there, Lord.

Day 15

Morning

In the dark night, O God, it is so hard to find the will to do anything. Yet how pointless it is to sit all day rehearsing, in deep despair, intractable problems, wallowing in worries, reliving anxieties. But this is what I do, Lord. I do not open a book. I do not switch on the radio to listen to music. I am not interested in the daily newspaper or anything that is going on in the world outside. The telephone is nearby but I have no wish to talk to anyone. There is just nothing that will lift me out of this mood. Life is . . . nothing. I simply exist . . . with a fingertip hold on reality. I do know that I still have to ring the bank, or further trouble will come. So I do not want to live, yet will do essential things in order to maintain life. I eat because I have to. I sleep because I can no longer stay awake. I look for glimmers of hope, Lord, but I find none. If there is hope, I do not feel it.

My closest friend has come to see me. For that I, reluctantly, give thanks. Would I like some books from the library? Shall I bring you my CD player and some CDs? How hard she tries to reach me!

How difficult it must be to try to break through such dismal moods.

How daunting it must be to face persistent 'No's to any positive suggestions. The reality is that, in my dark night, Lord, I am simply not interested in anything. For the efforts she has made, I can feel grateful. I know her intentions are all good. But I just cannot respond.

My family phone, but receive only the same negative responses. Again, I am grateful but I can do nothing. The dark night still enfolds me.

Evening

Thank you, O God, for those who try so hard to reach me and turn my attention to creative things. I so dislike my incapacity to respond to their promptings. But the depression is a reality. The dark night is intense.

But, once again, why am I offering a prayer of gratitude, Lord, when I can no longer reach you? What point is there in prayer when my prayers are never heard? Why should I pray when the answers I seek never come? And this is so, even if, as I have said before, I pray 'in the name of Jesus'.

The allure of sleep is cancelled out by the dread of waking. I repeat how hard it is, Lord, to face another day! What have I done in the past days but spent them being 'troubled and afraid'? Tomorrow will be no different, Lord.

What future is there if this dark night goes on and on and on, Lord? This is, I say it again – and will say it again and again – sheer desolation.

And in that desolation, I fall asleep . . . unwittingly, but with the words of a hymn running through my mind:

> Through the long night watches
> May thine angels spread
> Their white wings around me
> Watching round my bed.[22]

Would that it were so, but there are no angels here, Lord.

Day 16

Morning

The dark night has, indeed, come. Morning and evening and night are all alike (I use the word again): desolate. My sense of abandonment is very real. My God, my God, have you forsaken me? And why? My 'Calvary' is vastly less than Jesus endured, but his words express what I feel today. How can I face anything, derelict as I am?

I still do not want to meet people, speak to callers. I am not interested in the post, reading, music . . . the sense of emptiness is all-pervasive. I say again: who shall deliver me from this body of death? The hours pass slowly by as I sit alone in my room, as always pondering uselessly, worrying endlessly, still seeking answers to intractable problems, creating nothing.

'Come to your senses', they will say who think they know best, whoever they are. 'Snap out of it!' 'Show some will-power.' They simply do not understand, Lord. Call it, medically, depression or, spiritually, the 'dark night of the soul', such an act of will is impossible. All motivation towards good or growth is simply lacking. That is at the very heart of the problem. So I cannot 'snap out of it', however hard I try. I cannot get rid of the feeling of abandonment by pretending it does not exist. I cannot decide that my behaviour is absurd and consciously change it. This is an illness, be it psychological or spiritual. Medically it calls for medication. Spiritually it needs divine intervention.

But how can I ask for this, Lord, when you are not there?

Evening

The day that is ending, Lord, has been spent at my lowest ebb. And though I plead your name, I cannot pray. My mind too is tired: I cannot think properly any more. I have gone over and over the problems I face (have I, in my darkness, got them wholly out of proportion, Lord?) but all it leads to is a spiralling down into further gloom. How can I sleep tonight?

My closest friend came today, as she always does. For that I am grateful. She brought a book she found in a charity 'table-top' sale, a book by a noted artist, encouraging its readers to draw and paint.[23] It lies beside me, unopened. Perhaps in time I will read it, not now. The 'dark night' still stifles everything creative and worthwhile.

If I could pray, Lord, my prayer would be for sound sleep, freedom from bad dreams, and courage for the waking time. But it is no use, I cannot pray, Lord, for the 'tie that binds' me to you has broken.

I go over in my mind the words of benediction: 'The peace of God, which passes all understanding, keep your hearts and minds in the knowledge and love of God, and of his Son Jesus Christ.' Someone asked me yesterday what my favourite text was; I quoted this blessing. 'Fantastic,' he said. He is right.

But still I have no peace, Lord . . .

Days 17–40
Towards the light

Day 17

Morning

Will it be ever thus, Lord? So little sleep . . . So many waking hours. The dawn brings me no comfort, Lord. The early morning is still the hardest part of the day.

What is there now in life, Lord, that is worth anything? This is no more than existence. All that I used to know has gone. Anything I hoped for in life can no longer come. What desolation!

But why am I praying to you, Lord, I ask again? You are no longer present. Is it some basic instinct that compels me to turn to you, Lord? Or is it just use and wont, mere habit? I long for you to make your presence felt, but I feel it cannot be. The 'dark night' does not allow faith or hope. Or does it? Can you be found in the darkness, Lord?

The long hours of loneliness are in front of me again. I sit and think and worry and complain. About what do I complain, Lord? About the void in which you have left me, Lord. About the helplessness and hopelessness of my situation. I have nothing left to give. I am nothing.

The hours drift slowly by, with nothing done, nothing ventured, nothing gained. In desperation I pick up the painting book, the one my closest friend brought yesterday. She brought colouring pencils with the book. I open it up and choose a picture to colour in. Completed, I put it aside for my friend to see when she comes again.

Evening

It is evening time and, in the darkness that surrounds me, I feel a sense of gratitude that, for the first time since I 'descended into hell', I have achieved something, a rough painting. My coloured picture will do nothing to change the world, indeed it will not change anything. But at last something has caught my interest. For that, I give thanks, Lord.

Yet I still despair for the future. I still do not want to meet or talk to people. I still ignore calls to attend to urgent business. The post lies unopened. All I do is regurgitate my problems, yet finding no solutions. Has worrying become a way of life for me, Lord? Is it almost an addiction without which I cannot do? How awful, Lord, is this state of mind. How futile is this way of life.

Again, I find talking to you in this way is strange, Lord, for I have lost faith in you. I pray but no longer believe in prayer. Although I cannot sense your presence, deep down I feel that you have not closed the door to me. My grasp of you has gone, but your grasp of me, I do believe, still holds, Lord. As long as that remains, there is hope.

It is time to try to sleep. Even with medication, the side-effect of which is to encourage sleep, it does not come easily. Perhaps two hours will be possible, Lord, and then the long wait for the dawn. A dawn which, alas, I fear.

Day 18

Morning

As I awake, I realize a Christian colleague will come to see me today. Does he come at your bidding, Lord?

Apart from my family and my closest friend, I still resist visitors. Rehearsing my problems, describing my desolation, reliving my pain, as I have had to do so often with doctors, psychiatrist and others, are daunting prospects indeed. I feel guilty over my lack of gratitude for the trouble he has taken to come here, for the thoughtful concern shown by him. I just need to be alone in my 'dark night'.

It is my duty to reflect on my situation before my colleague comes. In my desolation, what can I do? What are my greatest needs? There is no spark in life at all. Everything is shrouded in darkness and gloom. I do not see how that darkness can be dispelled.

As I meditate in your presence, Lord, I recall a story about Robert Louis Stevenson when he was a boy, living in Edinburgh. He was looked after by a governess. He was thrilled to see the lamplighter come after dark with his long pole. 'Come and see this,' he cried out to his governess, 'there's a man outside punching holes in the darkness.'

I cannot do that, Lord. I have no energy, physical, mental, emotional or spiritual, for such a purpose. Only your intervention, Lord, will bring light into my dark place, But are you there, Lord, in the darkness? Don't the mystics say that that is where you can be found?

With feelings of apprehension, I await the visit.

Evening

For this day, Lord, I am grateful. I found it possible to ask my colleague to end his visit with prayer. A good and holy man he is; I grasped the opportunity to ask for absolution. The need for total forgiveness and assurance of it was very real. If I have difficulty believing in the reality of your presence, indeed existence, my colleague had no such problem. He listened, prayed and gave absolution in Jesus' name. I end the day a step forward, and with some sense of peace.

Thinking of this day's event, I feel a sense of hope. I have always believed, Lord, until this dark night came, that (as I have said) there was a covenant relationship between us: on your side, the covenant of grace, on my side, a covenant of faith. It is my part of the covenant which has failed. Can I retrieve it, Lord?

It is strange, Lord, but I dare to hope that a movement forward has been taken. Time will confirm if this is so. The dark night of the soul lasts a long, long time. I must wait on you, O God, in expectation.

And so I do. 'I wait for the LORD; my soul doth wait, and in his word do I hope.'[24]

Day 19

Morning

I wake and the dreaded morning hours are facing me. Has my mood changed? This is the aim of the anti-depressant medication. Perhaps it has, but the night of the soul remains very dark.

I thank you, O God, for the assurance of forgiveness given to me yesterday. Though I still find it difficult to feel your presence, the faith that others have encourages me. I know, Lord, that many good people are praying for me. For that I am grateful. I ask you to hear them, Lord, though you may not hear me.

My closest friend tells me that I have made progress. I did at least open, with some degree of willingness, the post she handed me. I had not done that before now. But still I want no contact with events or people. I still hold on to the solitude in which I wrestle endlessly and unsuccessfully with 'the problems'. The ring of the phone fills me with dread. I do not want to know who is there or what it is about. Only to my family and friend will I speak.

And so my journey towards the light goes on, but the light at the end of the dark night tunnel is not yet in sight. Could it be within the darkness itself that I first find some light?

Each day is still a struggle, Lord. As this one is.

Evening

O God, how deep depression can be! The doctors talk of 'mood' and wonder whether it has changed. On a scale of one to ten, they asked me some days ago, at what level did I feel myself to be? 'Five out of ten', I said, knowing that perhaps even that was pitched too high when I recall the depths of despair that I had when I reached crisis point. 'What will it take to get you back to ten out of ten?' the psychiatrist asked. I felt like saying, 'You tell me.'

I have heard it said, Lord, that there is a road that leads to hell, even from the very gate of heaven. But, more importantly perhaps, there is also a road that leads to heaven from the very gates of hell. It is that road I seek. But dark is the night, so very dark, Lord. Will it be within the darkness that I find you, I ask again.

They all say: 'It takes time', Lord. Then give me the strength to wait and hope, to take small steps along the way. I took one big step with the prayer of absolution. Can I now say six out of ten? Perhaps I can. And with that thought, I wait for sleep.

Day 20

Morning

The time to get up has come . . . and has gone. To lie in bed and think, think, think is painful. To get up and face the day is even worse. But I have no choice. I swap the bed for the chair . . . and continue to worry.

I recall the prayer of absolution and tell myself I must go forward. Backwards I must not go. I turn to my painting book again.

Newspapers have remained unread . . . I still have no interest in the outside world, but today a crossword catches my eye. I tackle it.

How difficult it is to break out of the circle of despair! What or who can help me to do it? My closest friend has come. We complete the crossword. She sees what I have done as a sign of hope, Lord. If it is, I am grateful.

Evening

'One more step along the world I go!' wrote my friend Sydney Carter, who died not so long ago. I am grateful, O God, for each faltering step through the darkness towards the light.

I used to expect miracles, O God, because your Word encouraged me to do so. How I need a miracle now! But faith has waned with my increasing doubt as to whether you are indeed 'God with me'. I still feel that sense of being abandoned. Lord, I do not know if you are near. Grant, therefore, that I may begin to see little miracles, 'divine surprises' . . . for they are as much 'wonders' as any dramatic event.

I have painted a little. I am solving crosswords. I have even begun to create my own crosswords. My attitude to the post now means that I am facing and dealing with external events. Perhaps these are, in their own way, little miracles.

I told the doctors today that I thought I could now say seven out of ten.

Day 21

Morning

Eight hours of sleep last night! How grateful I am for this. Is it the medication or your gift, O Lord? I put it down to both, for medical aids are part of your gifts of creation and are in your hands. The gift of sleep, however, does not take away the pain of facing a new day, Lord. It may in fact increase it as one emerges from the bliss of non-consciousness to the realities of life. Early morning is depressing for me, and I have still to overcome the 'down' feeling that it brings. Thankfully, Lord, as the day goes on, it will get easier. For that, too, I give you thanks.

It is mid-morning, Lord, and my closest friend has arrived. She brings a message that a long-standing colleague of ours has died in her nineties. I conducted her playwright husband's funeral just a few months ago. Can I take hers? Regrettably I cannot do it. At this stage of my illness and recovery it is not possible. Would I then write an obituary for the 'Other Lives' column in *The Guardian*? I felt bound to say that I would try to do that.

This afternoon, I wrote the tribute. For weeks now I have not put pen to paper to write anything, but to my surprise, Lord, I found that I had produced something that was worthwhile. My friend typed up the draft and sent it to Renata Symonds' family with a request for clarification and amplification of some facts and also the background to her long life. She was a refugee from the Nazis who came to England and became a psychotherapist. For over 50 years she had seen clients, right up to her death. Again I felt that I had taken a step forward.

Evening

I do not know whether you hear me, Lord, but I do want to give you thanks. Since I was a child, I have had the urge to write. When I was about 11, I received half-a-crown (as it was then called) for my letter to the editor of *The Children's Newspaper* – my first professional fee! I feared that in this dark night, Lord, my creative ability had been destroyed, but today's successful effort has helped restore some faith in myself and given me hope.

When forward steps are taken, how firmly must one hold on to them and establish them, Lord. One forward step will surely lead to another one. The dark night so destroyed all creativity that to recover some part of it is a ground indeed for rejoicing.

It has been a good day, Lord. Hope has been rekindled, some feel for life has been restored. When the obituary appears in *The Guardian*, as I greatly hope it will, it will speak to me of progress.

With that thought, I can now take my rest. Whether you hear me or not, I say 'Thank you', Lord.

Day 22

Morning

It is still not easy to face each new day, Lord. The will to survive is present all right, but the need to meet people and to deal with urgencies remains hopelessly weak. The realization that there are physiological reasons for the early morning depression is not enough to provide the positive attitude required to overcome it.

I deliberately pause, Lord, determined to remember the positive steps of yesterday, but the struggle to 'get started' remains overwhelming. You say, Lord, in your Word that 'those who wait upon the Lord shall renew their strength, mounting up with wings as eagles'.[25] I want to believe this, but my damped-down, nearly non-existent faith does not allow me that comfort.

I simply find it impossible to 'run and not be weary, to walk and not faint',[26] Lord. The motivation and the will to act are just not there, Lord.

The draft obituary returned to me today. Recognizing the envelope I opened it immediately, wryly aware that until now, during this dark night, I had totally resisted opening mail until I had to. The draft is fine, the family say, and they have added a few facts I had not known. I attend to the alterations and adjustments at once, again contrary to what I have been doing. I recognize the step forward and give you thanks, O God.

Encouraged by my handling of that specific task, I gratefully turn to others.

Evening

Thank you for this day, Lord. I realize again that I am turning to you although I feel, in my heart, you are not with me, you are not there. It seems as if I simply cannot let you go. I am still angry, Lord, that in my darkest hour you forsook me. You did not listen to my prayers.

When the dark night came upon me, Lord, all my ability to turn to you ceased, all my creative ability vanished, all my positive thought was ended. I am still in that dark night. I still feel forsaken, despairing, derelict, abandoned ... repetitive words, Lord, but honest words.

What can possibly break through this darkness, Lord? Will some event, one surprise happening, restore my faith? Will you reach out to me in the darkness in some unexpected way? I dare to hope you will.

And so to rest and to wait, Lord.

Day 23

Morning

I feel this new day will bring another step forward, O God. The dreaded morning hours make such a hope feel futile, Lord, but I try to cling to hope. Perhaps there will be a divine surprise today. Perhaps that step forward will take place.

The daily post arrives. Unwelcome as it is, I can now deal with it at once. It contains sad news, Lord. I learn of the death of a woman in her late middle life after serious illnesses and operations. It is her mother whom I know well. What a sorrow to befall her in her nineties! How difficult it must be to suffer the loss of a 'child' at that age. And since then, she has lost a grand-daughter too. This lady's firm faith and life-long discipleship will carry her through these losses, Lord, but what suffering for her . . . as well as for her son-in-law and their family.

It is all too easy, Lord, when the dark night comes, to turn to self-pity. How salutary then for me to have to think for a moment about others' pain. I need to write a letter of sympathy to this good lady today. It seems unfair that she should suffer so. That chimes in with my feelings about my own suffering. It, too, feels unfair, Lord. Have I not served you in ministry for a lifetime? Have I not done all I could to serve others in your name? Yet in my darkest hour you were not there, Lord. I asked but did not receive. I sought earnestly for, but did not find, solace or comfort. I knocked, but doors remained shut. It feels unfair, Lord.

Evening

Why do bad things happen to good people, like that mother, or myself? I do not, of course, count *myself* as 'good'. Far from it, Lord. With your servant Paul, I would classify myself as 'chief of sinners', but the question remains: why do good people (like this lady) suffer such great pain?

Before I rest, I think about this 'mystery of suffering', Lord. I still cannot bring myself to watch television or listen to the radio, but I do glance through newspapers. How men and women suffer! The pain of Iraq and Afghanistan with their multitude of deaths, wounds and destruction, the desperate poverty with all its terrible consequences that haunts Zimbabwe, the violence against protesters in Burma, wide areas of starvation in many parts of the world, the spread of AIDS in Africa, hurricanes, tornadoes, fires, earthquakes, tsunamis . . . one can go on and on. All these situations, and many more, I have brought to you in intercession, Lord, but massive suffering in all these places and others goes on and on and on. Will it ever be different, Lord? How long, Lord, how long?

The need to pray is very present with me, Lord, but the dark night remains and I find it difficult to do it. Yet where can I go to find solace and support? Would that someone comes to 'punch a hole in my darkness'.

Day 24

Morning

I am due to attend a group today, Lord, as part of my treatment plan. Depression brings complete withdrawal. You don't want to meet or mix with people. All you want is to be left alone with your misery to brood on problems, anxieties, worries. The effort to reverse that trend must begin, Lord. If today it is an effort, it can now be done. At seven out of ten, improvement has been noted, while willingness to associate with others is also seen as a sign of that improvement.

I am trying to be positive, recognizing that, while depression 'downloads' one's mood, it does not reduce mental ability. To help maintain that, I do every crossword I can find and continue composing them myself. I try to read, but still unwillingly. The trivia of fiction sits uneasily with the sombreness of the dark night, Lord. Be that as it may, a number of positive steps have now been taken. I am once again handling property problems that I have had to leave to my daughter during this dark phase. The strongest 'positive' is that I continue to write. For that, I am grateful, Lord.

The words of the hymn run through my mind and strike me with their relevance: 'I do not ask to see the distant scene, one step enough for me.'[27]

That is how it is, Lord.

Evening

For progress achieved today, I thank you, Lord. I came through the group ... a memory group ... with flying colours. I seemed to remember much more than the others who were there. There is no reason to boast about this! The group was made up of people with anxiety problems, depression, even some bordering on dementia, but rediscovering one's abilities does give some sense of satisfaction.

I thank you too, Lord, for the progress I felt I could report to the doctors and was pleased to find they agreed with my assessment. They look for improved 'mood' and are pleased with my social involvement. But the dark night is still with me. I do not know how to revive my faith so the prevailing sense of your absence persists, Lord. I wait, and hope for a 'divine initiative'.

The disciples were told: 'You have not chosen me: I have chosen you.' I pray, Lord, that an initiative from you may take place for me. I must be open to your Spirit, when the Spirit comes. If the door of my heart is closed and locked, you cannot enter.

Nor will you force your way in, Lord, for that is not your way.

I say: 'Come, Lord Jesus' and wait in hope and expectation . . .

Day 25

Morning

Another day, another group. Will this be a further step forward, Lord?

The time for the group has come. Waiting for it to start, I find myself on the fringe of a conversation . . . about you, God. A member of the group, less disturbed than others, has strongly affirmed his current belief (he used to believe otherwise) that there is no God. One of the helpers (N, one with whom I have found relationship difficult) rebuked him sharply. 'There is a God,' she said, with conviction, 'and he looks after me every day of my life. He has blessed my children and I know that he will always watch over us.'

N was a puzzle to me, Lord. She would sing gospel songs and choruses as she worked and was a keen church member. I felt we had common ground but, for some reason, she did not seem to like me. I don't know why. She only spoke to me if she had to, and often seemed to ignore me. Yet here she was making a personal testimony in a way that filled me with admiration as she continued to 'lecture' the group member on her faith, established a long time ago. I found myself moved by her words, Lord.

When she had finished and the recipient of her testimony had rather slunk away, I felt I had to thank her. 'Thank you for what you said, N. I was very impressed by it.' 'Since I was converted,' she said, 'I have served God every day and he has never let me down.' Then, looking directly at me, she said: 'Put your trust in him upstairs, Denis, and *don't worry*.'

Her words struck home, Lord.

Evening

I cannot wait for evening time and the time for prayer to come, Lord. You are real again. It was N's words that broke through the barrier.

So simple, yes, but everything was said in a way that makes them absolutely true. Here was someone willing to take you at your word, Lord, and she knew that all you said about faith and prayer was true.

This was a miracle! It was the event from outside me that could restore my faith. Be not troubled or afraid, indeed!

I take time to reflect on an incident that has touched me deeply, Lord. My uneven relationship with N was unimportant and irrelevant. She had, in a few moments, encapsulated the faith we shared and I was the beneficiary.

I said my prayers, confessed my faith and went to sleep.

Day 26

Morning

As always, the day begins with feelings of depression, but today there is a difference. I no longer doubt your presence, Lord, so you are with me in this difficult morning phase. N's words of witness have punched a large hole in my darkness, Lord. They give me real hope.

Having taken a few steps forward in these last days, I have new confidence as well as hope. While I know I have a need for solitude, I can now mix with others. I still, however, need reflection time, especially to think about yesterday's divine surprise.

Evening

I have accomplished much this day, Lord, with business done, letters written, writing tackled, future plans considered. For all this, I give you thanks, Lord.

I must reflect, Lord, on all that has happened in the last two days: what has changed, what hasn't. How do I now move from eight out of ten to ten out of ten? That is the point at which 'recovery' will be real. It is the point at which, in the continuing dark night, light will begin to be seen at the end of the dark tunnel. So there is still some way to go. The drop in mood will continue to be present each morning. It will still need an effort, aided by grace, not to be 'troubled and afraid'. I cannot yet face the world confidently, nor freely associate with people, nor be at ease with the ringing of the phone. Tasks I used to take in my stride will still be burdensome, and some of them may feel threatening. But I am ready to take life on again, Lord. That is where I am now.

And so, in this evening hour, I come to seek your help, Lord. Without your grace, I can do nothing. With it, all things are possible.

My grasp of you had gone. Your grasp of me still holds. Two days ago, I could not acknowledge that fact, Lord. Now I can.

And with that acknowledgement, I take my rest.

Day 27

Morning

Waking up, even now, is not easy, nor will it ever be, Lord. I do not expect the immediate future to be easy, Lord, but there is now hope for the future.

Life, however, is going to be different, Lord. I cannot go back to where I was, nor do I want to. The shape of things to come is far from clear. It is a time of uncertainty. But the fundamentals remain as they were. At the centre of all that I face is my vocation. This is to serve you, Lord. New ways of fulfilling that vocation must be found. The proclamation of the faith remains my primary task. It will certainly be much more with the pen than with the spoken word. How I do it will evolve slowly.

This is no time, Lord, for grandiose schemes. Physically and mentally I am tired. New strength has to be found. Emotionally I feel drained, having passed through a period of great stress and strain. You do not suddenly emerge from the dark night into bright sunlight. The way leads rather through decreasing darkness, and in that darkness I discern ever increasing light. In medical and psychological terms, medication must continue for a year, possibly two years, but with reducing doses. I earnestly pray that my future ways may be 'ways of pleasantness' and my paths be 'paths of peace'.[28] But I know these things are still some distance away.

And so to the work of today, Lord, whatever that may be. At least I am now ready to get it done.

Evening

It takes time to assimilate a miracle, Lord. I do not doubt that it happened. I need time to understand the full significance of what has taken place. I am, however, aware that a degree of peace of mind has come into my life.

This is the time to call on all the means of grace that you have so generously provided, Lord. It is a time for prayer, indeed for much prayer. It is a time for re-reading your Word and confirming from it the promises that you have made. I have lost the habit of worship: to that, and indeed to all these things, I must strenuously return.

It is, too, a time to draw on the support of others, particularly my family and closest friend, but also a wider circle of people who have been supportive of me by their cards, letters and prayers. Many things need to fall into place, Lord. Enable them to so do, I pray.

And so I leave this uncertain future in your hands, Lord. I accept the need for change that advancing years must bring. Help me to see the ways in which I can serve you still.

All this is positive, Lord, and for that I am grateful as I take my rest.

Day 28

·•◆•·

Morning

I wake up, immediately aware of the positive change that the last two days has brought. Not least is the fact that I can pray again, which I now do, Lord. I need to seek your constant help for this journey through darkness to light.

How great that need for help is in the early hours of the day. Negative feelings seep back into my consciousness; how dismal life can feel at 8 a.m., Lord. But with your rediscovered grace, I will triumph over these things.

Healing involves co-operation. You are the healer, Lord, but I must make an effort too. And I must look for ways of taking progress forward within your providential care. I must attend to business matters now and not neglect them as, when the dark night was at its worst, I was ever ready to do. There is writing to be done, both ministry and 'commercial'. I need to associate with people, to mix and mingle rather than always to seek to be alone. I need to lose myself in work: I have for too long put my problems at the centre of my life. I must stimulate my mind, learn new skills. Having passed through a time of simply existing, I need now to live with a future opening up before me. There is a lot to be done, but not all in one great swoop. One more step . . .

Strengthened, I go on my way . . .

Evening

Nightfall has come, but with some sense of satisfaction, Lord.

I have attended to business needs. I have drafted an article on 'The Angel of Amsterdam', Major Alida Bosshardt, who died last week. I have known her for a long time, having years ago been asked to write a popular life of this extraordinary Salvation Army officer, who worked for 27 years in the red-light district of Amsterdam. I have also spoken to several people on the phone, while tomorrow there is another group meeting. These may be ordinary things, but coming through the dark night, Lord, they are new to me. It is still dark, but achieving what I have achieved today speaks to me of progress, Lord.

I am the more grateful, Lord, for the unfailing support of my family and closest friend. I realize that they have shouldered the burdens arising from my withdrawal from the world into the dark night, burdens I am now able to take on again.

And so to rest. I shall sleep . . . the medication virtually ensures that that happens. What I need most is the strength to face the morning . . .

For that I pray this night, Lord.

Day 29

Morning

The morning gloom, that persistent feature of depression, has passed and the work for today has to be done. I again find myself thinking of articles that I could write. Some would be wholly in the context of ministry, Lord. Some would be for purely financial reasons.

Have I still the ability to do it? In the dark night all creative ability goes, but depression need not destroy such ability. It simply dulls down all motivation to do creative things. The return of the urge to write an article is another hole punched in the darkness and the will to do it is there. I have drafted an article on my experience of depression; I shall be interested to see the final result.

The day goes quickly by. No longer do I sit for hours in futile reverie. To be back 'at the desk' is indeed a sign of hope, Lord, for which I give you thanks.

I am not yet able to say 'ten out of ten', Lord, but I am on the way to it.

Evening

I come to evening time with something of a sense of peace, Lord. The day has brought some achievement and therefore some satisfaction. Confidence in my ability to write is returning. I have now also handled some difficult business matters without flinching. For all these small steps forward, I am grateful, Lord. The article on Bosshardt (she was almost always referred to simply by her surname) has been completed.

Tonight I feel a need to reflect more deeply on the significance of the darkness, Lord, the darkness in which I still am. Some words from the psalmist are speaking powerfully to me. He says: 'For the darkness and the light are both alike to thee'.[29] I am beginning to sense that it is in the depth of the darkness, 'a starlit darkness' as Helen Waddell calls it,[30] that light begins to break through. Is this, Lord, what the mystics call the *via negativa*, the negative way? When, in the sheer intensity of the darkness, a moment of opportunity for progress in the spiritual life arises? A feeling of your absence, far from being desolation, becomes a factor for good. The negative way is not a talking about your real absence but a very profound way of describing your overwhelming presence.

This makes some sense to me, Lord. Did not your servant Moses climb to the mountain top to draw near to the thick darkness 'where God was'?[31] Is not this 'the cloud of unknowing'? Is not your presence like 'a lightning flash which suddenly illuminates the darkness'?[32] If this is the point at which I am, Lord, I feel great hope.

It is never easy to go to sleep because of the fear of the morning, but it is a little easier tonight, Lord.

Day 30

———— ✦ ————

Morning

It is with a feeling of greater confidence that I greet this new day, Lord.
The underlying depression, so familiar at this time of day, is still there,
but a definite element of hope is now also present with me. I meet
the doctors today, Lord. Can I say a tentative ten out of ten, so far as
my mood is concerned?

The post is in. Business matters need attention, and there is personal correspondence to be dealt with too. I immediately set about
this task and accomplish it. That done, I must give my attention to
your work, my ministry, and plan how I can forward that.

One project begins to occupy my mind. Will it be a service to
others if I find a way to write about my dark night? Can I, by reflection on my own traumatic experience of that lonely, frightening
journey, help others, similarly suffering, to cope with their pain?

I write down the essential stages in my downward journey to
ultimate crisis, and then sketch out the long journey back towards
the light. I am still on that journey, Lord, and perhaps too close to
it to see the picture clearly, but there is material for thought in this
scheme. Time will tell if it can be brought to fruition.

How good it is to be thinking of future plans and possibilities. You
have indeed, Lord, as the psalmist said, 'given me back my peace'.

Evening

The day you gave, O Lord, has ended with genuine hope and calm
gladness. 'A tentative ten out of ten,' I told the doctors today, Lord.
They were pleased to hear these words and talked about terminat-
ing my treatment; I had made 'a very good recovery', they said.
I would formally be discharged from their care in a few days' time,
but medication and periodic checks would continue. The risk of a

relapse was again mentioned, but as a possibility, not an inevitability. They wished me well.

I am grateful to you, O God, for the degree of recovery I have achieved. But I must journey on through the darkness, which is easing but will be present still for some time to come. Every day must see some new forward step, something I am able to do that had, up to that point, proved impossible. More holes must be punched in the darkness. What new divine surprises will come?

My chief desire is to see clearly your guiding hand in all I undertake, Lord. When I am taking the right step, Lord, support me; when something I choose to do or plan is not according to your will, prevent me, Lord.

And so to rest, quietly and confidently . . .

Day 31

Morning

I awake, aware that I must continue to look forward, think ahead. That I know. All in all, I need to make progress towards the light at the tunnel's end. It will not be plain sailing by any means. Dips in mood will come, as the early hours unfailingly remind me, but with faith and conscious effort these will be overcome. What is important is that I co-operate with your healing work, O God.

A writing schedule must now be planned. Ministry has the priority in that schedule, with writing for financial gain only secondary. First, however, business letters must be written and then acknowledgements of cards and letters from people kind enough to send good wishes to me must be done. I must also not so fill each day that I neglect contact with other people: group meetings will continue from time to time. A balanced day is what I must aim for, with a proper mix of social intercourse and solitude.

I am not sure that I have it in me to produce another book. Even before this time of illness, I felt I had 'written myself out', but now, praise be to you, O God, I feel an urge to try and write about my dark-night experience, in the hope that my journey downwards to darkness then upwards and onwards towards the light may be of help to others on similar journeys.

Thank you, Lord, for stimulating my thoughts on these things. To find such positive attitudes within is encouragement indeed.

Evening

'Now the day is over,' as the hymn says, and 'night is drawing nigh', Lord. I cannot yet avoid feelings of trepidation as the time to sleep approaches. The memory of so many mornings of misery is hard to shelve. It makes each night difficult still. But a degree of calmness and confidence has come to me, bringing a sense of peace. With that, I can face the night.

I review each day's events, counting my blessings, Lord. I am beginning to see clearly your hand at work in the progress I am making. I lost that sense of your overarching care when the dark night descended on me. I felt that you were not responding to my prayers, even though I always offered them 'in the name of Jesus'. But divine surprises are beginning to come into my life and I see your hand clearly at work in events. I recall N's simple faith and her profound trust in you. I am deeply grateful for the impression that she made on me at a time when I needed that 'divine initiative'. For the first time since the dark night encompassed me, I have stopped worrying about both present and future. All things are in your care, Lord, and there they are safe.

Self-centredness has been an aspect of depression, certainly in my case, of which I have become aware. Since this happened, I have not felt the need to think of others. In the dark night, all interest in, and concern for, the world outside me was simply reduced to nothing. Now I find that I am praying for Iraq, for Afghanistan, for Burma's protesters, for Zimbabwe's awful poverty, for reconciliation in the 'holy land'. I welcome this change in attitude, Lord.

All in all, I am relearning the fundamentals of my faith, namely love for you and for my neighbour.

And all this is in response to you, O God, who 'first loved us'.

Day 32

Morning

How can I serve you more through the ministry of writing, Lord? This is my waking thought. I see this as the main focus of my future ministry. The traditional role of preacher is less easy to fulfil as age advances. To that function I have given 65 years. Now my sermons must be proclaimed through the ministry of print. Perhaps I should begin today to try and write some sermons with a view to wider publication. My article on Bosshardt is ready to go to a high-circulation journal. I hope it will find a home there. After all, she is a sermon incarnate.

The possible book now takes priority in my future plans. I think it should be in the form of daily prayers, one for each morning and one for each evening. It is best that I leave the matter there meantime and commend the project to you, Lord. If it has your blessing, I will surely know.

I think again of the doctors' warning that relapse is all too easy, especially at the time of felt recovery. I do not think in those terms, Lord; I want to leave the dark night behind for ever and give the remainder of my life to committed service to you, to learn to enjoy pleasant aspects of life, to watch my great-grandchildren grow and develop.

I surprise myself with such positive thinking, Lord, but this is where I am – and where I want to be.

I go to my desk . . .

Evening

I am tired, Lord, not with worry but with work done. The Bosshardt article has gone and a first sermon drafted. Some further thoughts about the book have been written down. For all this, I thank you, Lord.

My family – that is my daughter and my son – have both been in touch again . . . they live a considerable distance away from me. They will try to come and see me soon. A ministerial colleague and his wife called today. He has had two long spells of depression, so knows the kind of experience I am having. As always, my closest friend has been to be with me. I did not hesitate at all in dealing with the urgent business matters she put before me (she has been looking after many things for me during this dark period). All these are encouragements, O Lord. I pause to give you thanks for them.

My mood is good too, Lord. When negative thoughts, fears and anxieties enter my mind, I pray to you to give me the strength (to use a rugby phrase) to 'kick them into touch'. One cannot help thoughts entering one's consciousness. It is what you do with them that is all-important.

Tired I may be, but I have some sense of contentment. And so I sleep . . .

Day 33

Morning

How important it is, Lord, that in the morning moments of depression, I fall back on my faith in you. In that period of reflection, I need to weigh up the realities of life, what is good and what is not so good, to 'count my blessings' and renew my resolve to go forward. The last two months have been so dramatic, indeed traumatic, that it will take some time to adjust to life as it is going to be. So much has changed from the structure of the life I had – the public work I had to undertake, my involvement in various organizations, etc. The coincidence of illness and my advancing age will make a more restricted life necessary, but it need not be less positive. Nor must my commitment to your work, Lord, be reduced: indeed, rather the reverse, it must increase. What has become clear to me in recent days is that writing will be at the centre of what I do. In that context my plan to write the book will be crucial.

I have lived life in the public eye for many years, but the time to leave that behind has come. It will be a more solitary life, but family and friends must be part of it. There is much that I can no longer do, Lord, but there are many other things I can do . . . and must.

I am still feeling my way through the thick but dazzling darkness. 'Do you see yonder shining light?' said Evangelist to Christian in John Bunyan's *The Pilgrim's Progress*. 'Yes, I do,' said Christian. 'Then make for it,' said Evangelist. I can see 'yonder light' at the end of the tunnel and I do strenuously make for it.

I settle down to send off the Bosshardt article, finish off an article on 'depression in the morning' for possible use in a national weekly, draft a contribution on improving football for a sports paper, and take time to think further about the book.

It is good to be busy again, Lord.

Evening

'Prayer is thinking about things in the presence of God,' said the preacher at morning worship today. It is more than that, Lord, but that element is certainly part of prayer.

In the evening quietness I think about the continuing journey towards the light. I see how I lost hold of my faith through feelings of abandonment and forsakenness. I was grieved, Lord, and indeed hurt that my prayers 'in Jesus' name' were not answered when I sorely needed your help. When problems were mounting daily, Lord, you did not seem to want to listen to my desperate pleas. Was I wrong in my approach to prayer, Lord? Were the answers I sought my will, but not yours? Was I wholly responsible for all that was going wrong, creating my own self-destruction? To all these questions, I give considered thought tonight, Lord.

The answers are still to be found, Lord, but I can at least think about them calmly and objectively. What is more, and very important, is that my rediscovered faith assures me of your presence at all times. As N said so simply: 'Trust him upstairs, and *don't worry*.'

I won't, Lord.

Day 34

---·•◆•·---

Morning

'May grace, mercy and peace from Father, Son and Holy Spirit be with you.' Aware of the dip in mood that always comes at this time, I stay with these words of benediction, Lord. It would not be difficult to descend into deep depression in these early hours, but bolstered by the blessing in these opening words, I face the day boldly.

There is much to do today in terms of creative work. I must therefore take on the pressures of life and apply myself to what I have to do. Thankfully, the motivation to go forward is now getting stronger each day. For this, I am grateful, Lord.

I want now to tackle the book, but despite last night's positive reflection, there is still some fragility within me over this task. Having to live through the crisis again seems too demanding, Lord. I'm simply not sure if I am ready to face that. I will give it a day or two's further thought.

I do feel able to tackle the sermons, Lord. They do not present me with the same problem. I will prepare those I have planned and hope that they will be accepted by a national journal. That would take whatever message they carry out into the world. I see my responsibility to proclaim the Word very clearly, Lord, so I must make every effort to do just that. What I have to do is begin! I do that right away.

The task goes well. I have completed the first sermon and will work on two more tomorrow.

Evening

Thank you for the encouragement of the day just ended, Lord. Today has helped me with my doubts over my mental ability. I now know it remains intact. I have wondered too if my spiritual strength was enough to produce worthy material: with my crisis of faith, I feared that strength had gone. The opposite, however, is the case. All I have gone through has, in fact, enhanced my faith. To know that this is so is a 'divine surprise' indeed! It is so good to realize that, as ageing reduces physical power, it can increase spiritual power. I find that encouraging, Lord.

But in one area of life there is risk, Lord. It is not thoughts but feelings that can pull you down. It would be easy to look back and become 'emotional' over what might have been and could have been, but there is no gain in following that track. I cannot tell where the path not taken would have led. I know the path taken. The reality is the here-and-now. It is with the future that all potential lies.

I have reached the stage – a further step forward – when I can lie down to rest with some sense of peace. I am full of gratitude, Lord, for the little, and sometimes very big, miracles you bring to me along the way. Divine surprises, indeed!

Before I sleep, I take time to plan tomorrow, for certain work must be done. The sermons need to be completed and a first draft of the proposed book must be attempted. Because I have spent a lot of time in my life writing to deadlines, I prefer the pressure such limits bring. For 13 years as editor of a national religious weekly, *British Weekly*, I had to write comments and leaders against the clock, while for another 13 years I had to provide a pastoral article for the same paper on time. More recently I had to write a weekly meditation in the *Daily Telegraph*, again for 13 years. So facing deadlines is not a burden but a help. What gives me pleasure, Lord, is that I am doing now what so recently I could not do, and that is thinking about tomorrow. That is progress indeed.

Day 35

Morning

That I have a programme for the day already in place makes the morning easier. It is still impossible not to feel 'down' at this stage of the day, but I am able to handle it more confidently as improvement continues. For that, I give you thanks, O God.

I also give my thanks for the reasons that I believe lie behind this improvement, Lord. What I have undergone in this dark night is a spiritual stripping that has led to a resurrection of my faith. Everything I believed came into question: belief in providence, in prayer, in the truth of the Incarnation, for you were no longer 'God with us', God with me, in the presence and power of the Holy Spirit to help, to heal, to sanctify. Things no longer 'worked together for good'. I had been left 'comfortless', Lord. Words like abandonment, dereliction, desolation came to reflect where I was. Then you sent a 'divine surprise' to open my eyes and show you to be 'unfailing love'. From there on, although the steps have been slow and to human eyes may have seemed trivial, the essential change in direction had taken place. Sensing the light which is in the 'dazzling darkness', I had begun the journey towards the full light at the end of the tunnel. Again, I give you my profound thanks, O God.

The daily routine is now pretty much in place, Lord. First comes correspondence and attending to business matters. It is my policy to deal with incoming mail on the day it arrives, but the sheer size of the post makes it impossible to do that on some days. I am finding, Lord, that with the endless demands associated with my public life now ended, I can deal with almost everything by return. Then there are business and other telephone calls. These too I handle confidently now.

Those matters dealt with, I can tackle the two remaining sermons slowly.

It is satisfying indeed to reach targets, Lord, and, in so doing, to serve you.

Evening

Another satisfactory day, Lord. To feel that one has something to give brings genuine pleasure. Having lost all sense of personal worth, stumbling through the darkness of the night, it is joy indeed to re-discover positive attributes and a sense of purpose. It is with that perception, Lord, I come to rest tonight.

One does not need to be clinically depressed to experience swings in mood. It is part of the experience of life to have 'ups' and 'downs'. Only when such swings become extreme does the label 'manic-depression' begin to apply. With clinical depression, the swings are more defined than they are in normal life. A major slide downwards is always a possibility. What makes me ponder this question now, when things are progressing, Lord? It is the need constantly to real-ize that I need your help.

But all is presently well, Lord, even if I reflect a little nervously on the proposed content of the book. Am I yet prepared to go through the painful memories of all that has happened to me? I must still assess this apprehension, so a further wait before my decision is taken is needed. But I can tackle the third sermon, Lord. If I can complete that it will be work well done. I know what the theme will be. It will be 'encouragement'. I know in whom I can find a prime example of encouragement. It is the great Old Testament figure, Nehemiah. He personifies for me 'the ministry of encouragement'.

For now, rest calls. For the degree to which I can now 'lay me down in peace', I give you thanks, O Lord.

Day 36

Morning

To awaken feeling a great sense of purpose is a blessing indeed, Lord. The dark night destroys all sense of meaning and purpose. It leaves you in limbo, with a sense of 'nothingness'. At its worst, the dark night was hell and there was no comfort in looking to the future, for there was no future. That is why finding some sense of purpose again means so much, Lord. It feels like resurrection.

But what a dark and gloomy morning it is, Lord. That does not help the early morning depression! It only makes it all the more imperative to wait upon you, Lord. In that spirit, I wait upon you now.

To help me cope better, I think of things that Jesus said: 'My peace I give to you; not as the world gives do I give to you. Let not your heart be troubled, neither let it be afraid.'[33] I recall too, Lord, those marvellous words of St Paul which I have already quoted: 'May the peace of God that passes understanding keep your hearts and minds through Christ Jesus'. 'Hearts and minds', 'knowledge and love' – how I value these words, that emphasize thinking and feeling with their counterparts in knowledge and love. And, of course: 'Be still and know that I am God,' as the psalmist says so movingly. All these are indeed 'comfortable words'. How greatly they help to bring some serenity amid the stress and pain.

If I am to fulfil the programme I planned, I must 'get moving' now, Lord! Post dealt with, business done, I turn to Nehemiah. If all goes well, some 90 minutes should see another sermon written. The sermons can then go off to the journal I consider is their right destination. Will they be accepted, Lord? That matter I leave in your hands. As Gamaliel said so rightly of all undertakings, if they are 'of God', they will succeed. That is enough for me, Lord.

Evening

For another day of achievement, O God, I give you thanks. The destiny of the sermons is, strictly speaking, in the hands of the editor of the journal to which they have gone. My perspective is wholly conditioned by my belief in your providential care. Whatever you will, will surely be done. I therefore leave them in your hands, and happily await the disclosure of your will.

The word 'sermon' has a traditional feel about it. To many it will be an old-fashioned and dated word. We live in an age of dialogue not monologue, many will say. People do not want a dogmatic declaration from 'six feet up'. That view I understand, Lord. Drop the word 'sermon' if it no longer speaks relevantly of communication, but do not discard the great truth behind it, namely that, call the method what you will, your Word must be expounded to the people.

I look back to my call, Lord. It was to ministry, to preach and (in Jesus' name and by his power) to heal. I cannot lay aside that responsibility. The exposition of the Word is as important today as it ever was. St Paul's words almost haunt me, Lord, so compelling do I find them. 'Woe is me,' he said, 'if I preach not the Gospel.' It can be by voice, it can be in print. But it must be done.

I surprise myself, Lord, with the vehemence of my thoughts on this matter. And I see my sense of commitment to 'preach the Word' in print as a further step forward.

As I prepare for sleep, I give you thanks for that, O Lord.

Day 37

Morning

I awake as yesterday, determined to fulfil the planned work for today. My desire to write the book which will help people with their dark night is pressing itself upon me. It must be a book of prayers, Lord, one for each morning, one for each evening of the days and nights of darkness. Can I help others cope better with their dark night? I hope so, Lord. I am convinced this is what you are asking me to do.

How greatly the call to work eases the depression of each morning. I wonder if that morning gloom will ever cease, Lord. I earnestly pray that it will.

I hurry to get business done, correspondence answered. The need to create the final plan for the book feels urgent now, Lord. I am doubtful over its length. I am sure that I must reduce the time-span considerably. Over 700 prayers would be needed on my present plan of a year. I cannot sustain that amount of input on such a specific theme.

The nervousness I had over reliving my dark night is easing, Lord. I think I can now face the past because of my present sense of peace. With that comfort, I long to begin. But for another night, I leave it 'on the table', Lord, or more properly, at your throne of grace.

I hope tomorrow will bring answers to my questions about the book. Sufficient now to 'take it to the Lord in prayer'.

Evening

What a pleasure it is to have one's mind full of future projects and plans, Lord. The balance between ministry and personal needs must be maintained. Ministry must have the first priority in all I do. Mary's choice, listening at Jesus' feet, was approved by him, but Martha's role is important too. We need something of Mary *and* Martha in our

approach to life. After all, 'Seek first the kingdom' is Jesus' clear statement of that which has first claim on a disciple, but the 'other things'
must get appropriate attention too. This is not a matter of allocation
of time but of attitude of mind. I cannot dismiss the need for financial gain, Lord, but that must never get in the way of ministry.

The time for evening prayer has come, Lord. If prayer is, as I quoted
several days ago, 'thinking about things in the presence of God', then
meditating on such priorities is time well spent. My object in life is
clear. It is to fulfil your will, expressing that purpose in committed
service to you and to other people.

I hope, Lord, that by tomorrow it will become clear what the
shape of the book must be. In psychoanalytic terms, I leave it to my
'unconscious' to wrestle with it while I sleep, but with my religious
perspective I also pray that you, O God, will be within the process so
that whatever the result will be, it will be 'according to your will'. As
I drift towards sleep, I pray: 'Thy will, not mine, be done.'

Day 38

Morning

But what will its format be? Must it be in the form of prayers? Morning and evening? What is the central purpose of the book? For whom am I writing it?

I must give considerable time to these matters today, Lord, but the structure of the day must be retained. Post and correspondence must be dealt with first. Some phone calls must be made. The second half of the day must then be given to reflection on the book, and possibly a very sketchy draft of its schema put down on paper.

As I was pondering the coming day, Lord, I realized how different life must now be. For many, many years I have served you in response to that call I received so dramatically over 65 years ago. I had no choice but to respond to that call with a firm 'Yes, here I am, send me!' But it was a willing 'Yes', one which, however hard times have been, I have not regretted. The coming of the dark night, whatever its causes, has reinforced that sense of vocation. The faith I have rediscovered will help me to find the new ways in which to fulfil it. To expound and declare the Word is what I am called to do, Lord.

Prepare me, therefore, for the vicissitudes of this new life. When my spirit droops, sustain me, Lord. When I move forward, bless me.

Evening

For the ordered, creative day that I have spent, I thank you, Lord. For my understanding of the proper balance between work and leisure, my thanks, Lord. For the combination of solitude and involvement (with family and closest friend), I praise you. For time spent reflecting on the book, I bless you, Lord.

As this day moves to its close, Lord, I thank you for the sense of providential care which has returned to me. You are indeed 'God with me'. I sense your presence in the way everything is evolving, in the purpose which you are shaping for me, in the possibility of my producing a book. In the dark night, all these thoughts were knocked out of me. How reassuring, Lord, it is to feel they have returned.

It is back to the book, Lord. A year of prayers is much too long, as I suspected. I need a shorter compass. I turn to the thought of using the period of Lent as a basis.

Tomorrow, Lord, is decision day, so nurture my thoughts during the hours of sleep and grant me on waking a clear picture of what I have to do.

I leave it in your hands, O God.

Day 39

Morning

Facing each new day is becoming easier, Lord. I know that intimations of despondency will continue to affect me in the early hours of each morning, but I must learn to cope with that. That there is now a sense of purpose to each day is a great help. I must continue to find purpose in life and this, with your help, Lord, I will do.

'Thinking in your presence', Lord, I reconsider the shape and content of the book. My most recent idea was the possibility of making it a book for Lent but now I am not sure that that will work. Lent books go on the booksellers' shelves for Lent, but lose their impetus when Lent is over. Because this is for ministry, commercial factors must not play a primary part. The question is whether a book built around Lent and its sequence will give me the framework in which to declare my message. In some ways it would, Lord. The Lenten period is a journey leading to the crisis of Calvary and it is followed by resurrection, but I think I want to embrace a longer period of triumph for there are dangers in that period for victims of depression, not present in Jesus' risen period. To try to force the sequence into that specific framework would not be ideal for me, but the length of time is about right. How about '40 days and 40 nights' for my journey into the dark night and out of it? I want, rather, to describe the journey through depression to healing so I think I will make the title 'Reaching Towards the Light'.

I am sure I am on the right track, Lord. Thank you for that.

Evening

For a profitable day, I give you thanks, O God. Work has been done that had to be done. The format of the book is taking shape in my mind. And altogether, there is a normality about the day just ending that is wholly encouraging. The feeling I get, Lord, is that the end of the tunnel is just ahead of me, and that once again I shall 'walk in the light'. For all that, I give you thanks, Lord.

I can now see that there are lessons to be learned from all I have experienced, Lord. One is the damaging effects of anxiety. Jesus said, according to the King James Version's rendering of Matthew 6.34: 'Take no thought for the morrow.' What I find helpful about the New English Bible's translation of that text is the introduction of the word 'anxious' into Jesus' statement. The significance of that word is important. There is no real point saying: 'Take no thought for the morrow.' We must plan ahead – and there are parables of Jesus making that point. It is not sensible future planning which is the subject of Jesus' words. It is looking to the future in an anxious, worrying way. Such anxious anticipation is not part of the Christian perspective, Lord. Being (to repeat the phrase) 'troubled and afraid' leads to negative equity in the soul. The Christian's outlook will be calm, serene, tranquil and confident, all qualities arising from a strong inner sense of peace.

It is not easy, Lord, to banish all worry and fear, but it is an obligation so to do. That is why you call us to a life of prayer, Lord.

> So let my walk be close with God,
> Calm and serene my frame.

Day 40

<hr/>

Morning

'Towards the Light: Prayers through Depression to Healing'. I awake, clear in my mind about the title and shape of the book. By travelling my journey into the darkness, sensing the light in the 'dazzling darkness' of the crisis, then following the slow, gradual but successful journey into the light, I hope all who meet depression will be greatly encouraged. Through grace and faith, this is a battle that can be won. On this basis I will start writing today, Lord.

The word 'cured' is medically inadvisable, but to speak in terms of 'healing' is proper and right, Lord. 'Healing' is the word I would use to describe my own recovery from depression. The possibility of a further episode, again slipping downwards into anxiety and fear, is always there, as the doctors have said and I have already noted. But that need not happen and should not happen. The medication will continue, but more important, Lord, is that I have a strong faith, one that has been refined through suffering that spiritual stripping of which the saints and mystics speak. My confidence lies in the resources of my faith, and on these resources I will draw heavily.

And so another day slips into gear, Lord. I open the post without hesitation. I answer the phone without apprehension. If I have to, I answer the door. These are everyday things but things I could not do in my fear and anxiety. Now I take them in my stride. Life is enjoyable again. There is some pleasure in being alive.

The time to write the book has come. I do not fear reliving the dark experience now that I know the story ends in the light.

I type up the title: *Towards the Light: Prayers through depression to healing*. It feels right to me, Lord.

Evening

I come to you, this night, O God, with thanksgiving in my heart.
For my recovery from depression,
   I give you thanks and praise;
For passing through the dark night and emerging into the light,
   I give you thanks and praise.
For family and closest friend who, at a cost to themselves, bore the
   burdens that I could not bear and, despite me, held my life
   together,
   I give you thanks and praise.
For those who sent letters, cards and flowers to encourage me,
   I give you thanks and praise.
For the many, far and wide, who prayed constantly for me,
   I give you thanks and praise
For doctors, consultant and other medical staff who planned and
   carried through my treatment,
   I give you thanks and praise.

But above all else, I give you thanks and praise
   that you never let go your grasp of me:
   you brought about decisive divine surprises;
   you punched great holes in the darkness
   and led me towards and into the light.

Your love, O God, is a love that simply will not let us go.

I pray for all who are passing through the dark night of the soul, and
   carrying the burden of depression. May they too move onwards
   towards the light.
   Through Jesus Christ, my Lord, Amen.

Afterword

Readers of this prayer diary might like to know how the three crises referred to in the Foreword as the cause of the depressive episode ended. The very large sum of money involved in the fraud was not recovered and never will be. The disastrous consequences of this were very hard to bear because, ultimately, mine was the blame for allowing the situation to develop. That reality had to be accepted and I had to 'move on'. The property crisis was, wholly miraculously, resolved without serious financial implications. The personal crisis had to be worked through and was. The cost of it all is in the story that has been told, a story that, happily, ends in victory.

Notes

1 Ephesians 3.17 (*New English Bible*). Where no particular translation of the Bible is listed, the references are in the author's own words, but these are always based on the King James Version.
2 Isaiah 1.18 (*New International Version*).
3 Psalm 139.5 (*New International Version*).
4 2 Timothy 1.12.
5 The noted Scottish theologian, author of *A Diary of Private Prayer*, *Invitation to Pilgrimage*, etc.
6 Psalm 139.8–12 (*New International Version*).
7 Philippians 3.14 (*King James Version*).
8 John 14.13.
9 Psalm 102.1 (*King James Version*).
10 Philippians 4.7.
11 Psalm 51.3 (*King James Version*).
12 Psalm 51.10–11 (*King James Version*).
13 John 16.33 (*King James Version*).
14 2 Corinthians 4.8–9 (*New International Version*).
15 Hosea 11.4.
16 John 20.29 (*New International Version*).
17 Matthew 11.28 (*King James Version*).
18 Psalm 121.4 (*New International Version*).
19 Psalm 107.28.
20 Romans 8.38–39.
21 Romans 7.24 (*King James Version*).
22 The hymn 'Now the Day is Over' by Sabine Baring-Gould.
23 Alwyn Crawshaw, *The Half-Hour Painter* (London: HarperCollins, 1989).
24 Psalm 130.5 (*King James Version*).
25 Isaiah 40.31.
26 Isaiah 40.31.
27 From the hymn 'Lead, Kindly Light' by Montague Augustus Toplady.
28 Proverbs 3.17 (*King James Version*).
29 Psalm 139.12 (*King James Version*).

30 Helen Waddell, *The Desert Fathers* (New York: Vintage Spiritual Classics, 1998), quoted by Melvyn Matthews in *Both Alike to Thee* (London: SPCK, 2000).

31 Exodus 20.21 (*New International Version*).

32 Melvyn Matthews, *Both Alike to Thee*.

33 John 14.27 (*New King James Version*).